The Transition of
Doodle Pequeño

A play for audiences of all ages by

GABRIEL JASON DEAN

Dramatic Publishing Company

Woodstock, Illinois ● Australia ● New Zealand ● South Africa

*** NOTICE ***

©MMXIII by
GABRIEL JASON DEAN

Printed in the United States of America
All Rights Reserved
(THE TRANSITION OF DOODLE PEQUEÑO)

For inquiries concerning all other rights, contact:
Paradigm Agency
360 Park Ave. South, 16th floor
New York, NY 10010 • Phone: (212) 897-6400

ISBN: 978-1-58342-854-2

IMPORTANT BILLING AND CREDIT REQUIREMENTS

All producers of the play *must* give credit to the author of the play in all programs distributed in connection with performances of the play and in all instances in which the title of the play appears for purposes of advertising, publicizing or otherwise exploiting the play and/or a production. The name of the author *must* also appear on a separate line, on which no other name appears, immediately following the title, and *must* appear in size of type not less than fifty percent (50%) the size of the title type. Biographical information on the author, if included in the playbook, may be used in all programs. *In all programs this notice must appear:*

"Produced by special arrangement with
THE DRAMATIC PUBLISHING COMPANY of Woodstock, Illinois."

"There came a time when the risk to remain tight in the bud was more painful than the risk it took to blossom." (*Anais Nin*)

ACKNOWLEDGMENTS

My process is deeply influenced by my collaborators and so this play owes many debts of gratitude. First and foremost, this play would not have been possible without Suzan Zeder, who patiently helped me stay true to the spirit of *Doodle Pequeño* and the kids in the quad. My immense thanks to Abra Chusid, Steven Wilson, Wendy Bable at People's Light & Theatre, Kim Peter Kovac and Deirdre Lavrakas at the Kennedy Center, The Youth Ensemble at A Red Orchid Theatre, Robyn Flatt at Dallas Children's Theatre, Sherry Kramer, James Still, Andrew Hinderaker, Alexis Scott and Jessie Dean. And to Karen Rodriguez, the original Valencia: *gracias por ayudarme con el español.*

FOREWORD BY SUZAN ZEDER

It's a wonderful thing when a writer discovers his or her voice. It's even better when that voice has something important to say for or about children. But it is best of all, when that writer is one of my students and that discovery happens in my class. It has been my great pleasure and privilege to introduce Gabriel Jason Dean to the world of Theatre for Young Audiences and now to write this introduction to his play *The Transition of Doodle Pequeño*.

At the end of the first semester of the first year of the MFA program in playwriting at the University of Texas, we ask our students to submit a portfolio of plays consisting of all of the plays they wrote before coming to us and all of their work in the first semester. In the dozen or so plays that Gabriel Jason Dean submitted, I noticed a fascinating pattern. Virtually every play featured a child or young character as a pivotal force in the dramatic action. None of these plays were intended for young people and indeed all of the child characters in Gabe's plays were in great peril, facing huge obstacles, often at the hands of adults. The children in Gabriel Jason Dean's adult plays dwell in dangerous places physically and emotionally and survive (or don't) by their wits, their courage and their humanity. What excited me most, however, was the fact that Gabe's theatrical worldview included children as citizens of the drama and subjects worthy of our attention and respect.

The Transition of Doodle Pequeño is Gabriel Jason Dean's first play written specifically for a young audience. In this play, he has tackled some serious subjects: bullying, gender identity and the isolation faced by children of immigrant parents. This journey into the child space of Doodle and his imaginary goat, Valencia, has brought him rich rewards as a writer: humor, fantasy and a love of language whether it be English, Spanish or Goat. In the years to come it will be fascinating to see if Gabriel Jason Dean's adult plays will continue to sophisticate and deepen his plays for young people and how his plays for children will bring the light of laughter and imagination to even the darkest places.

Isn't it exciting to be at the beginning of something wonderful?

7

The Transition of Doodle Pequeño was first presented on November 30, 2011, as a workshop production by the University of Texas at Austin Department of Theatre and Dance in the Oscar G. Brockett Theatre, directed by Steven Wilson and featuring the following cast:

Doodle .... Rene Castro
Reno.. Isaac Gomez
Valencia...Karen Rodriguez
Marjoram .... Uyen-Ahn Dang
Toph...Jacques Colimon
Baumgartner ....Rudy Ramirez

The University of Texas at Austin workshop production was created in collaboration with the following artists:

Stage Managers....................... Sarah Naderi & Victoria Solorio
Assistant Director .... Sam Gorena
Dramaturg...Abra Chusid
Composer... Randy Maguire
Sound Design...Stephanie Busing
Charge Scenic Artist... Emily Haueisen
Technical Director ....Dave Vieira
Scenic Design................. William Bloodgood, Mason Baker, Daniel Berkowitz, Nicole Ciesinski, Samantha Hong, Hannah Milem, Christen Perez, Danica Salazar & Bich Vu
Costume Design.......... ....Susan Mickey, Hope Bennett, Rebecca Bost, Haley Box, Emma Dirks, Jennifer Garrison, Josie Hood, Lily Matthews, Josh Miller, Payal Patel, Elise Romero, Catherine Solheim, Nickie Temprachanh, Vanessa Villareal, Morgan White & Chin-Hua Yeh
Lighting Design ....Michelle Habeck, Melissa Brown, Jordan Kirby, Natasha Rice, Kristen Thompson, David Toro, Dawn Wittke & Danielle Wright

The University of Texas at Austin production was then presented as a staged reading at Dallas Children's Theatre in February 2012.

The Transition of Doodle Pequeño was presented as a rehearsed reading in May 2012, at the Kennedy Center for Performing Arts, as part of *New Visions/New Voices* in partnership with People's Light & Theatre in Malvern, Pennsylvania, directed by Wendy Bable.

Winner of the NETC Aurand Harris Award and the Kennedy Center ACTF Theatre for Young Audiences Award

Runner-up for the Kennedy Center ACTF Mimi and Harold Steinberg National Playwriting Award

The Transition of Doodle Pequeño

CHARACTERS

DOODLE .... a fifth-grade boy
VALENCIA .... Doodle's imaginary goat
VOICE OF MAMÁ .... voiced by Valencia
RENO .... Doodle's fifth-grade neighbor
BAUMGARTNER .... a mysterious old man
MARJORAM .... a sixth-grade tomboy
TOPH .... a third-grader, Marjoram's little brother

CHARACTER NOTES

The vocal inflection of a native "Goat" speaker sounds a lot like a Mexican accent. In fact, maybe they're even the same.

< > is a beat for the actor.

The Voice of Mamá should be performed live offstage by the actress playing Valencia.

SETTINGS

A quadruplex in Southern California on Halloween.

AUTHOR'S NOTE

The first time I experienced a production of *The Transition of Doodle Pequeño* with a group of 8- to 12-year-olds in Austin, Texas, I was a big bundle of nerves. *Doodle Pequeño* is my first play for young audiences and it pushed me as a writer much more intensely than previous plays for adults. Who knew it would take a sassy goat to help me understand that I not only should take responsibility for my play, but also for the conversation it creates? That November night in the back row of the Oscar G. Brockett Theatre as the lights went down, I'm sure a few more gray hairs blossomed on my temples. But when the peals of infectious laughter began, I relaxed and went along for the ride.

At the play's conclusion, we held a discussion and asked, "What is this play about?" Many eager hands shot up. Friendship was the ubiquitous answer. I couldn't agree more. But the friendship that blossoms between Doodle and Reno is sadly not always the reality for people with gender-identity questions. I don't wish to oversimplify things and convey that everything "gets better" when gender-questioning kids find a friend. At the end of this play, I don't know what the future holds for Reno and Doodle, only that they are at the beginning of something new.

In addition to being a celebration of the possibility of friendship, I hope *Doodle Pequeño* is a story that asks the audience to examine labels, question pejorative terms and understand the deleterious consequences of misused language. Words have the power to enslave and destroy. But when examined with open hearts, those same words possess the ability to free and restore us. It's also about actions—how simple kindnesses might save us—sharing an orange, teaching a song, attempting a new language, or trying to understand someone instead of mocking him because he's different.

I hope the play will be as meaningful to you as it is to me.

July 19, 2012

12

The Transition of Doodle Pequeño

AT RISE: *The jack-o'-lantern 6 o'clock Pacific sun is be-*
ginning to set on a hilltop stucco quadruplex in Southern
California. Leafy trees in the courtyard cast eerie shad-
ows. The Santa Ana winds blow and we hear the low
murmur of many wind chimes. BAUMGARTNER, wearing
a nuclear waste-style getup with a fumigating mask,
grumbles through the courtyard. He's fertilizing plants,
weeding his beds, examining his trees and hanging a few
Halloween decorations.

(DOODLE, wearing his school uniform and a backpack,
sprints into the courtyard, seemingly carried by the wind.)

DOODLE. Trick-or-treat! Smell these feet! Gimme some-
thin' good to eat! If you don't, then I don't care … *(For-*
gets words.) If you don't, then I don't care …
BAUMGARNTER *(peeking out from a bush).* I'll pull out
your ugly hair! *(Laughs raucously.)*

(The wind howls. DOODLE and BAUMGARTNER regard
each other. DOODLE runs toward his apartment. BAUM-
GARTNER watches him. Lights rise on DOODLE and
Mamá's cramped, one-window, studio apartment crammed
with unpacked boxes. A message machine lets out a lonely
beep.)

DOODLE. ¡Mamá! ¡Ya llegué de la escuela! < > ¡Mamá!
   < > Oh no.

(DOODLE presses a button on the message machine.)

VOICE OF MAMÁ *(via the answering machine)*. Hola,
   Doodle Pequeño. This is Mamá. Are you home? < >
   Ohhh … lo siento mucho, cariño. La otra cajera renunció
   hoy. Y ahora tengo que cubrir su turno. < > I know, mi
   amor, you are going to be angry, pero este trabajo nuevo
   nos va a ayudar a pagar los gastos. Pero, llegaré a casa by
   nine of the clock—
DOODLE. You promised—
VOICE OF MAMÁ. I so sorry, niño. Pero, I bringing *25*
   PayDay candy bars home para tí— *(To customer.)* I be
   right with you, sir. Necesito regresar a trabajar, Doodle.
DOODLE. I want to go trick-or-treating. Like normal kids!
VOICE OF MAMÁ. Llegaré a la casa a las nueve—
DOODLE. All the candy'll be gone by then!
VOICE OF MAMÁ *(to customer)*. One second, sir. Doo-
   dle—I almost forgetting—por favor, take the monies up-
   stairs to the landlord.
DOODLE. That man is super scary!
VOICE OF MAMÁ. Él es muy agradable. Ahora eres big
   boy. La renta se tiene que pagar hoy.
DOODLE. You're the adult! You pay for things. Not me.
VOICE OF MAMÁ *(to customer)*. I be right with you, sir.
   Oh, estoy emocionada por verte en tu disfraz de diablo!
DOODLE. I'm not wearing that stupid devil costume!
VOICE OF MAMÁ. < > Doodle … things will be better for
   us.

(Singing.)
  NARANJA DULCE
  LIMÓN PARTI—

(BEEEEEEEEP! DOODLE slumps, unwraps a PayDay candy bar, eats it miserably.)

VALENCIA *(from inside the cabinet).* B-eh-eh-eh-eh-eh!

(DOODLE casually opens the cabinet and VALENCIA, the goat, emerges.)

VALENCIA. Hola hola, Doodle Pequeño …
DOODLE. Hola, Valencia.

(VALENCIA takes the PayDay from DOODLE, chomps it.)

DOODLE *(cont'd).* Heeey—por qué estas eating my candy bars? Aren't you supposed to be eating grass or something?
VALENCIA. Ay, give me break. I *your* imaginary goat. I eat what *you* eat, mijo.

(DOODLE slumps.)

VALENCIA *(cont'd).* Ay, you are one cloudy little Doodle.
DOODLE. I hate this stupid place so stupid much! We haven't unpacked yet! I've been wearing the same underwear for *three days*! I am not paying the stupid rent! *(Finds his devil horns, tail and bow tie. As he speaks, he rips them up.)* Y no voy a ir a stupid trick-and-treat o usar estos cuernos estúpidos estúpidos!

VALENCIA *(stomps and kicks some boxes which fly across the room).* Espera. Why are we so much angry?

DOODLE. Mamá's stupid job!

VALENCIA. Stupid stupid stupid! Wait. What does that mean?

DOODLE. It means we hate it.

VALENCIA. Stu-u-u-u-u-u-u-pid!

DOODLE. Mamá's going to be mad at us.

VALENCIA. These things could be worse. *(Scratching herself.)* At least *you* no have fleas. < > Ah, maybe instead of your devil horns, you wearing my horns instead.

(VALENCIA lifts her horns off her head, places them on DOODLE's head. DOODLE giggles in spite of himself and VALENCIA goat-leaps.)

VALENCIA *(cont'd).* You be the goat. I will be the *chupacabra*!

DOODLE. Chupahuh?

VALENCIA. Chupacabra. You know, mijo … goat vampire.

DOODLE. Vampire?

VALENCIA. Sí. The chupacabra comes out at night when cabritos like you are asleeping. He bites them on the neck with his muy grande fangs—

DOODLE. Fangs!?

VALENCIA. Sí, and then he drinks all their blood like it was Kool-aid! < > Mwah-ah-ah-ah-ah!

(Silence.)

VALENCIA *(cont'd).* Now, you be the goat.

DOODLE. Why do *I* have to be the goat?

VALENCIA. Because you wearing the horns.
DOODLE. < > Fine. But *no* biting!
VALENCIA. Yeah, yeah. OK. Now, channel your inner goat.

(DOODLE strikes his best goat pose.)

VALENCIA *(cont'd)*. This is your best goat?
DOODLE. Yeah, what's wrong?
VALENCIA. Goats have four legs.

(DOODLE goes down on all fours.)

VALENCIA *(cont'd)*. That's a little better.

(VALENCIA adjusts DOODLE to make him more goat-tastic.)

VALENCIA *(cont'd)*. Sí, now you are a real goat.
DOODLE *(unconvincingly)*. Bah-ah-ah-ah-ah.
VALENCIA. Más o menos. Now, pretend you are asleeping.

(DOODLE snores.)

VALENCIA *(cont'd)*. Cierra los ojos!
DOODLE. If I close my eyes, then you'll attack me.
VALENCIA. Sí.
DOODLE. I don't wanna be attacked.
VALENCIA. Are you scared of the chupacabra?
DOODLE. No!
VALENCIA. Then, cierra los ojos!

(DOODLE closes one eye.)

VALENCIA *(cont'd)*. Both eyes!

(DOODLE nervously closes both eyes. VALENCIA hides in a small box. A loud grinding noise comes from the courtyard where BAUMGARTNER is fiddling with an uncooperative machine.)

DOODLE. Valencia? What is that noise? Valencia? *(Opens his eyes, looks around for VALENCIA.)* Valencia?

(DOODLE goes to the window to investigate the noise and sees BAUMGARTNER.)

BAUMGARTNER. Blasted technology!

(VALENCIA emerges from the small box and stalks behind DOODLE chupacabra-style. VALENCIA looks as though she is going to ferociously bite DOODLE's neck. DOODLE turns to see her.)

DOODLE. AHHHHHHHHH!

(VALENCIA goes for DOODLE's neck, but instead of biting him, she makes a fart noise on his neck with her lips.)

DOODLE *(cont'd)*. Hey! Hey! No flurbling, Valencia!
VALENCIA. ¿Qué?
DOODLE. No flurbling my neck meat.
VALENCIA. What is *flu-u-u-u-u-rbling*?
DOODLE. Farting on my neck.

(VALENCIA flurbles DOODLE. DOODLE flurbles VA-LENCIA.)

VALENCIA. Be-eh-eh-eh-eh-eh!

(DOODLE chases VALENCIA! She goat-leaps on boxes, chairs, counters. They chase until they are out-of-breath exhausted.)

VALENCIA *(cont'd)*. Ayaya! The sugar from the PayDays making me bouncing off the floors!

DOODLE. You mean bounce off the walls—

VALENCIA. BAHFOOGEE.

DOODLE. What did you say?

VALENCIA. < > Bahfoogee.

DOODLE. Is that Spanish?

VALENCIA. No. It's Goat.

DOODLE. You speak Goat?

VALENCIA. Por supuesto, Doodle. I am goat, so I speak goat.

DOODLE. What's it mean?

VALENCIA. It's a curse word in Goat. Not meant for cabritos like you to be hearing.

DOODLE. I'm not a cabrito anymore. What's it mean?

VALENCIA. Is a b-a-a-a-a-a-d word to say—como when you lose something importante. I say it when I mixing up my Goat and English phrases. When I *lose* my words. I say it lots of the times.

DOODLE. Teach it to me!

VALENCIA. < > You can no say it front of Mamá. Do we have a deal?

DOODLE. Deal.

VALENCIA. Repite, por favor: *BAAAAHHHHFOOOOGEEE!*
DOODLE. *BOOOOOOOOOOFAAAAAAAAAAHHHHGEE-
EEEEEEEE!*
VALENCIA. Um, your accent's a little funny. It sounded
like you saying I have a big nose.
DOODLE. You do have a big nose.
VALENCIA. Besides the point. < > Try again.
BAAAAAAHHHHHFFFFFFOOOOOOOOOGEEEEEEEE!
DOODLE. *BAAAAAHHHHFFFFOOOOOOGEEEEEEEE!*
VALENCIA. Very good!
DOODLE. *BAAAAAA—*

*(BAUMGARTNER grinds in the courtyard. DOODLE and
VALENCIA cautiously approach the window. The two are
amazed by BAUMGARTNER's every move. He smashes
something underfoot, picks it up and examines it.)*

BAUMGARTNER. Looks like your run-of-the-mill Drosphila melanogaster. Not a Drosphila suzukii, thank
goodness. *(Ritualistically puts things from the grinding
machine into his sprayer.)* A bit of bone meal, kale, clay,
shark fin, garlic—

*(BAUMGARTNER pours a red liquid from the machine
into his sprayer. He slowly drags a big ladder across the
courtyard. It makes horrendous noise. He climbs, grum-
bling with every step. He stands on top of a ladder,
grunting and spraying the trees with a frightening mist.)*

DOODLE. *WHAT* … is that? Is it el chupacabra?
VALENCIA. No, it's worse. It's the *L-A-A-A-A-A-ANDLORD.*
DOODLE. What do you think he's *doing*?

VALENCIA. He say something about bones.
DOODLE. So?
VALENCIA. Maybe he's doing an ancient vo-oo-oo-oo-oo-oo-doo magic spell cursey thingy. Maybe he's a *brujo*?
DOODLE. Witches are usually girls.
VALENCIA. Boys can be witches, too.

(A gust of wind. BAUMGARTNER is shaky on the ladder. Wind chimes roar.)

BAUMGARTNER. BWAH! Confound Santa Ana! Stay in Mexico!
DOODLE. I don't think I can give him the money.
VALENCIA. You no pay, we no stay.
DOODLE. ¿Y qué? This place is a dump.
VALENCIA. This place is our new casa, Doodle Pequeño!
DOODLE. You sound like Mamá.
VALENCIA. Fine. This place is stu-u-u-u-u-upid.
DOODLE. Much better.

(VALENCIA kicks a box across the room. DOODLE throws a small box marked "fragile." Major breakage.)

VALENCIA. Oopsy. Mamá is going to grind us for good.
DOODLE. *Ground* us.
VALENCIA. BAHFOOGEE.

(DOODLE picks up the box.)

VALENCIA *(cont'd)*. If you no open it, then you can deny it was you.
DOODLE. Sí, tienes razón. *(Hides the box in the cabinet.)*
VALENCIA. Out of the mind, out of the sight.

DOODLE. No, out of sight, out of mind.
VALENCIA. Ay, Bahfoogee!

(DOODLE stares worriedly at the cabinet. After a moment, he opens the cabinet and pulls out the box.)

VALENCIA *(cont'd)*. Ay, Doodle. No abras esa caja.

(DOODLE pulls a bit of the tape off the top. VALENCIA gasps and shudders. DOODLE pulls again.)

VALENCIA *(cont'd)*. Be-eh-eh-eh-eh-eh-eh!

(DOODLE pulls again. VALENCIA faints.)

DOODLE. You are so dramatic.

(DOODLE digs inside the box, spilling packing peanuts on the floor. VALENCIA suddenly uprights.)

VALENCIA. Oooooo—what are those?
DOODLE. Peanuts.
VALENCIA. ¡Ay, delicioso! *(Eats one, violently spits it out.)*
DOODLE. ¡No, cabra tonta! Packing peanuts. For to pack things.
VALENCIA. Yuck! Phew! Ewwwww. Gr-o-o-o-o-o-ss!

(VALENCIA takes the box, dumps it. A broken picture frame falls out. DOODLE picks it up. It's a photo of DOODLE, Mamá and Papá.)

DOODLE. Oh no. *(Sitting.)* Oh no.

VALENCIA. Who is that funny-looking muchacho? He looks like you with a mustache.

DOODLE. Ése es mi papá.

VALENCIA. I never meet this papá.

DOODLE. He's in México.

VALENCIA. ¿Por qué?

DOODLE. He didn't have the right papers.

VALENCIA. For to eat?

DOODLE. No. For to stay. < > I can't believe we broke this!

VALENCIA. *We*, big man?

DOODLE. Sí, we!

VALENCIA. No, no, no, Doodle Pequeño. I am no real. How can I be breaking things? *(Picks up another packing peanut, eats it.)* Is an acquired taste. Be-eh-eh-eh-eh.

(A loud knock on the door. VALENCIA goat-leaps onto the countertop.)

VALENCIA *(cont'd)*. Expecting a visitor?

DOODLE. No.

(Another knock.)

VALENCIA. You should maybe be thinking about answering the door.

DOODLE. Mamá says never open the door a los extraños.

VALENCIA. How you know is a stranger?

DOODLE. Do *you* know who it is?

VALENCIA. You are the only person I am knowing, Doodle. So how do I know?

(More knocking. For longer this time.)

VALENCIA *(cont'd)*. I no think this stranger—who may not be a stranger— is leaving.

DOODLE. Ay, what if it's el brujo wanting his money?

VALENCIA. Pues, you give him the monies!

(DOODLE carefully approaches the curtainless window, hoping not to be seen. Suddenly, RENO, dressed in full old-school vampire regalia, appears in the window.)

DOODLE *(screaming)*. AAAAAAAHHHHHHHHH!

RENO *(screaming back)*. AAAAAAAAHHHHHHHHHH!

VALENCIA *(bleat screaming)*. B-EH-EH-EH-EH-EH-EH! < > Espera. Why are we screaming?

DOODLE. El vampiro at our window!

VALENCIA. ¿Chupacabra?

DOODLE. No—vampire … like a regular people vampire.

RENO *(knocks on the window and holds up his trick-or-treat bag)*. Trick-or-treat?

DOODLE *(yelling)*. Mamá says I can't open the door for strangers.

RENO *(yelling)*. I'm not a stranger.

DOODLE. How do I know?

RENO. Because I live here. *You're* the new kid. *You're* the stranger.

DOODLE. You *look* strange.

RENO. I'm in your class at school!

DOODLE. You are?

RENO. Yeah, I look different without the cape.

(DOODLE opens the door slightly.)

RENO *(cont'd)*. Trick-or-treat!

(RENO is wearing a ballet tutu.)

DOODLE. ¿Qué se supone que eres?

RENO. What?

DOODLE. What are you supposed to be?

RENO. I'm Count Chaos, a vaudeville vampire.

DOODLE. What is that?

RENO. Vaudeville was a type of theatrical entertainment popular in the days of old.

DOODLE. < > You're wearing a dress.

RENO. Tutu actually.

DOODLE. It's still a dress.

RENO. So?

DOODLE. You're a boy. I think.

RENO. I think so too.

DOODLE. You *think* so?

RENO. Yeah. < > But vaudeville vamp, she's definitely a girl.

DOODLE *(to VALENCIA)*. No entiendo—

RENO. In vaudeville, boys dress like girls and vice versa. < > So—trick-or-treat?

DOODLE. I don't have any candy.

RENO. What's that goat eating then?

DOODLE. ¿PUEDES VER MI CABRA?

RENO. I don't speak—

DOODLE. *YOU* CAN SEE MY GOAT?

RENO. Duh. I have an imagination too.

VALENCIA & DOODLE. ¡Ay, dios mío!

(VALENCIA flurbles RENO.)

VALENCIA. That is what's known as a flurble.

RENO. Cool.

(RENO flurbles VALENCIA.)

VALENCIA. Cool.

(RENO almost flurbles DOODLE, but DOODLE puts a hand up to stop him.)

RENO. What's your name again?

DOODLE. < > Doodle.

RENO *(laughing)*. That's what my grandpa calls it when the cat misses the litter box. A *doodle*. The cat's really old. And kinda blind. I'm Reno.

VALENCIA. Like the city in Nevada?

RENO. Totally.

VALENCIA. Mi nombre es Valencia. Nice to be meeting you, Reno like the city in Nevada.

RENO. B-eh-eh-eh-eh-eh-eh-gup.

DOODLE. You speak Goat?

VALENCIA. Actually—he speaking Sheep.

RENO. They sound similar. I used to have an imaginary sheep.

VALENCIA. Used to?

RENO. The Santa Ana winds blew Sigmund away last year.

(A big gust of wind.)

VALENCIA. I be staying en la casa. Just in case.

RENO. Soooo—about that candy—

VALENCIA. Want a PayDay?

RENO. Um, does a goat have horns?

DOODLE. No, not every goat has horns.

RENO. Ohhhhh—OK … *(Grabs horns from DOODLE's head.)* Mister Smarty Pants Kitty Doodle—now they do.

(RENO puts the horns on VALENCIA. VALENCIA laughs and tosses RENO a PayDay.)

DOODLE. ¿Por qué te estás riendo?
VALENCIA. Oh, I laughing because he said—he called you a … never mind.

(BAUMGARTNER grinds.)

VALENCIA *(cont'd)*. < > Reno like the city in Nevada, what's that noise?
RENO. You mean … the troll?
VALENCIA. ¿Un ogro? We thought he was el brujo.
RENO. El what?
DOODLE. Witch.
RENO. Does he look like a witch?
VALENCIA. Oh, this is no good. I knew a troll once. Very temperamental.

(BAUMGARNTER grinds louder.)

VALENCIA *(cont'd)*. What's he doing?
RENO. Grinding little boy bones for his pumpkin trees.

(VALENCIA faints. DOODLE catches her.)

DOODLE. Those are not pumpkins! Those are naranjas!
RENO. Come again?
VALENCIA *(waking)*. Oranges.
RENO. They are *definitely* pumpkins. Blood pumpkins. Trust me.

(The three move to the window to watch BAUMGARTNER.)

RENO *(cont'd)*. The blood pumpkins are for evil children.

VALENCIA. *¿Evil* niños?

RENO. Bullies and pranksters ...

DOODLE. ¡Mentiroso!

RENO *(overlapping)*. *And* the troll makes evil children swallow the blood pumpkins WHOLE!

VALENCIA. B-eh-eh-eh-eh-eh-eh! They no choke?

RENO. The pumpkins make your belly stick way out like a basketball. And it churns and turns until all the evil is gone. Sometimes it lasts for days—*weeks—YEARS*!

VALENCIA. How you knowing so much about this troll?

RENO. Back in the day when I was a first-grader, there was a boy in my class who lost his two front teeth and every time he talked, he *(whistling)* whistled.

(VALENCIA laughs.)

RENO *(cont'd)*. Beware of laughing, Valencia. I laughed and made up funny names for the whistling boy, which I won't repeat because one night as I was sleeping, the troll yanked me out of bed, dragged me by my hair and made me swallow *three* blood pumpkins—*AT THE SAME TIME*!

VALENCIA. Say is no so!

DOODLE. ¡Qué estúpido!

RENO. You wouldn't want to find out, right?

VALENCIA. No, no, no! We no want to be finding out.

DOODLE. How can you believe this payaso?

VALENCIA. This clown is very convincing.

RENO. Believe what you want, but don't say I didn't warn you.

DOODLE. Whatever.

RENO. It's your funeral. < > So why aren't you dressed up, *Doodle*?

DOODLE. Porque no. < > Halloween is for weirdoes. Like you.

RENO *(paces around the apartment, sizing up the place)*. I'm the weirdo, huh? Don't you think fifth grade's a little late to have an imaginary friend?

VALENCIA. Cut him break. He just moving here. Sometimes you needing the imaginaries when you going through the tough times.

RENO. You moved here from Mexico?

VALENCIA. Sí, he come from—

DOODLE. Shhh!

VALENCIA. ¿Queeé?

RENO. It's cool. I mean, I just thought 'cause you don't speak English—

DOODLE. I speak English! I'm speaking English now!

RENO. Oh, I'm sorry, I mean because you speak Spanish—

DOODLE. I moved here from the East Side! I was born here, OK!

RENO. It's cool, Doodle. Wherever you came from. < > When I moved here—that's when I found Sigmund.

VALENCIA. When he come here, Doodle reaching out the car window and hooking me by the horns and pulling me inside. Tell him, Doodle.

DOODLE. No quiero.

RENO. < > You live here *alone*?

DOODLE. I have a mom!

RENO. Not everybody's so lucky.

VALENCIA. Mamá's at work. She just got a job at a convenience store. It's convenient for everyone but us.

RENO. Where's your dad?

DOODLE. You ask too many questions!

RENO. Geez—I'm just trying to be friendly. < > Fine. You ask me something.

DOODLE. Why you wear that dress?

RENO. Tutu.

DOODLE. OK. *Tutu.* < > It's not normal.

RENO. Neither is an imaginary goat.

VALENCIA. Hey hey hey. Be nice.

DOODLE. Boys shouldn't dress like girls.

RENO. < > I do sometimes.

DOODLE. Even when it's not Halloween?

RENO. < > Yeah.

DOODLE *(laughs)*. Whoa. That's … that's weird.

RENO. Yeah. It is. Kinda. I guess. So?

DOODLE. I bet you get made fun of all the time.

RENO. I don't wear dresses at school. Do you take your goat to school?

(VALENCIA sadly shakes her head. RENO takes off the tutu.)

RENO *(cont'd)*. Wanna try?

DOODLE. No, gracias.

VALENCIA. Ooo—oooo! I will! Me me me! < > Hey, me por favor!

(RENO gives VALENCIA the tutu. VALENCIA twirls!)

VALENCIA *(cont'd)*. I feeling so fancy. *(Goat-leaps and frolics.)* Doodle! You should be trying this! Come on—it's so much of the funs!

(VALENCIA makes it too hard to resist. DOODLE caves, tries it on.)

DOODLE. This is kinda dumb.
RENO. Twirl.
DOODLE. No!
RENO. Just twirl.

(DOODLE half-heartedly twirls.)

RENO *(cont'd)*. Now with gusto!

(RENO takes DOODLE's hand and spins him. Spin, spin, spin. DOODLE laughs.)

RENO *(cont'd)*. Really fun, right?
DOODLE. < > It's not so bad.
RENO. Hey! Maybe you could go trick-or-treating with me!
DOODLE. I have to wait for Mamá to get home.
VALENCIA. She is no getting here till nine.
RENO. Whoa! All the candy will be totally gone by then.
DOODLE. Sí, I know, right?
RENO. We'll be back before nine. Your mamá will never know.
DOODLE. Pues, I don't think—
VALENCIA. We could get the candies—
DOODLE. She's already gonna be mad because we broke stuff.
VALENCIA. But the ca-a-a-a-andies!
RENO. You know, rolling with Reno has its privileges.
VALENCIA. O-o-o-o-o-o, privileges!
RENO. I know all the candy hot spots. This one lady on Carson gives out king-sized Reese's Peanut Butter Cups!

King-sized Reese's Peanut Butter Cups. Just saying it makes your mouth water.

(They imagine the king-sized candy.)

DOODLE. I don't have a costume.
RENO. No problem … amigo.

(RENO opens a box marked "Las ropas." He wildly throws clothes around the apartment. VALENCIA joins in.)

RENO *(cont'd, holding up a Davy Crockett hat)*. What about this?

(VALENCIA is appalled.)

DOODLE. Too much dead animal.

(More rummaging.)

RENO *(holding up clown wig)*. What about this?
DOODLE. Too much rainbow.
RENO *(holding up a pirate sword)*. What about this?
DOODLE. Too … Espera un momento. That's … ¡perfecto!
RENO *(holding up a bandana)*. And this! Tie it on your head. You could be a pirate!
DOODLE. Ése es Papá's.
RENO. He won't mind.
DOODLE. Give me that. *(Holds the bandana. Puts it on his head.)*
RENO. You look totally cool. *(Holding up a flowery skirt.)* What about this?
DOODLE. It's a dress.

RENO. It's perfecto!

DOODLE. It's Mamá's.

VALENCIA. She won't be minding. You can be she-pirate.

DOODLE. I don't wanna be a she-pirate. Doodle is a he-pirate.

VALENCIA. But Reno like the city in Nevada is wearing a tutu.

DOODLE. Reno is … special.

RENO. Hey—the troll will hear you. He's like Santa Claus. He hears everything.

DOODLE. Lo siento, pero I'm not wearing a dress. < > It's *stupid* and it's *gay*.

(RENO leaves without a word. BAUMGARTNER slowly follows RENO through the courtyard.)

VALENCIA. You have hurt Reno like the city in Nevada.

DOODLE. ¿Y qué? He's a weirdo.

VALENCIA. You are having an argument with a goat. You are weirdo too.

DOODLE. Pero, he's a boy and he wears girl clothes!

VALENCIA. He was our friend.

DOODLE. We work better alone.

VALENCIA. You saying something before—una palabra … a word … it was a curse word in human … How you say it? Ga-a-a-a-a-ay? < > What this curse mean?

DOODLE. It's not a curse word.

VALENCIA. You say it like one.

DOODLE. It's … it's—you wouldn't understand. It means raro … weird. Or stupid. Like a boy who wears girls' clothes.

VALENCIA. I thinking is weird you wear clothes at all. I no wear the clothes and nobody is minding.

DOODLE. Animals don't wear clothes.

VALENCIA. You are animal.

DOODLE. I don't have fur to keep me warm.

VALENCIA. You no need to keeping warm. Vives in sunny California!

DOODLE. I have to wear clothes! And they have to be pants. No skirts with stupid flowers on them.

VALENCIA. Says who?

DOODLE. Says the whole world.

VALENCIA. Even the whole world can be wrong, Doodle. I thinking you should apologize. You make Reno like the city in Nevada sad.

DOODLE. You are *my* imaginary cabra. You are supposed to *agree* with me.

VALENCIA. Says who?

DOODLE. Says me!

VALENCIA. OK—I am liberated goat! I am free to express my own opinions.

DOODLE. Your opinions are gay.

(VALENCIA kicks a box. It flies!)

VALENCIA. Take that back, Doodle Pequeño.

DOODLE. No.

VALENCIA. Take it back or, te prometo, I will charge.

DOODLE. Stupid stupid smelly gay goat!

(VALENCIA charges! Headbutt! Goat battle! It's epic. As they fight, RENO walks matter-of-factly through the courtyard. VALENCIA pins DOODLE against the wall.)

VALENCIA. Reno's your only friend. He wants to take you trick-and-treat. He tells you about the horrible blood pumpkins. He is helping you for to make a new costume after you rip yours— *(Bends DOODLE over her knee, spanks him.)* Tenga, tenga, tenga, tenga, tenga ...

(RENO enters without being invited, doesn't close door behind him. He carries his tutu in hand.)

RENO. If it makes you feel better, I won't wear the tutu. < > Oh, um, uh, sorry. I can come back later—
VALENICA *(releasing DOODLE).* Is OK, Reno like the city in Nevada. < > You want to be saying something, Doodle?
DOODLE. Um. Yeah. It's cool. I guess. Because it's Halloween. *(Grabs his skirt, puts it on.)* I'm ... I'm ...
VALENCIA. You are Prin*cess* Peg-leg and he is Count*ess* Chaos.

(RENO and DOODLE consider their new names.)

RENO. Sweet! Let's crush this quadruplex's candy supply! Brought you a bucket.

(A burst of wind through the door.)

VALENCIA. Oh no! I can no go to trick-and-treat! Santa Ana will be blowing me away like it did the Sigmund!
RENO. You can hold onto me.

(Another wind burst.)

VALENCIA. I stay here. < > I can no risk it.

(Before DOODLE closes the door, he looks back to see VALENCIA. DOODLE and RENO exit into the courtyard. The moon is rising. For the first time, we see blossoms on the trees and huge orange orbs hanging from the limbs.)

DOODLE. Whooooooooa!
RENO. Dare you to pick a pumpkin.
DOODLE. Me?
RENO. No, the other pirate princess.

(DOODLE looks behind him.)

RENO *(cont'd)*. Double dog dare you!
DOODLE. Pero—
RENO. Triple dog!!!
DOODLE. I don't have a dog. I have a goat.
RENO. It's a dare, Doodle.
DOODLE. Pero—
RENO. Don't be a punk.
DOODLE. You said name calling makes the troll angry.
RENO. Punk isn't so bad. Come on! Pick a pumpkin. Halloween deserves as many tricks as treats.
DOODLE. What's in it for me?
RENO. Fame. Fortune. Bragging rights for infinity.
DOODLE. No sé. What if—
RENO. I thought you weren't scared of the troll.
DOODLE. I'm not.
RENO. So pick a pumpkin. The window of opportunity's closing, Peg-leg. You *could* be a legend.
DOODLE *(giving Reno his pirate sword)*. Hold this.

(DOODLE quietly pulls the ladder to the tree, carefully climbs and struggles to remove one of the biggest orbs. TOPH, a cowboy bandit, rushes onstage whirling a pumpkin flashlight.)

TOPH. Put 'em up! Give me all your candy! Give me those chocolates, your caramels, your gummies, your sours, your toffees and brittles, candy corns, tootsies, lollies and jawbreakers, chewing gums, malted balls, vanilla chocolate strawberry lime, any flavor's fine. Except licorice. I hate licorice. *(Spits, cowboy style.)*

DOODLE. You didn't say anything about the pumpkin police.

RENO. I didn't know.

TOPH. Hand over the goodies, fellows.

RENO. Get out of here, Toph.

TOPH. Who is this Toph character of which you speak?

RENO. This is Toph. Toph meet Doodle.

TOPH. Oh, so you're the new kid in the quad. < > The Candy Bandit is growing impatient. Now—hand over the goods! I ain't afraid to shoot.

RENO. Scram, Yosemite Sam.

TOPH. Aww, come on, Reno … I'm just fooling. Can't you play along? < > What are *you* supposed to be anyway?

RENO. I'm a vaudeville vampire and this is Princess Pegleg.

(TOPH roars with laughter.)

DOODLE. What's so funny?

(TOPH is still roaring.)

DOODLE *(cont'd)*. What's so funny … you, you—

RENO. Punk!

DOODLE. Punk!

TOPH. You're wearing dresses! *(Laughs.)*

(MARJORAM, a tomboy, enters. She is wearing everyday clothes, except for her t-shirt which reads, "This is my costume.")

MARJORAM. Who are you harassing now, you little nightmare?

TOPH. They're ... they're wearing—look at 'em—they're wearing dresses!

MARJORAM. So what?

TOPH. But—they're boys.

MARJORAM. So?

TOPH. Well—you know.

MARJORAM. It's Halloween. < > So, it's OK to dress different today.

TOPH. Oh yeah. Right.

MARJORAM. Little brothers are so stupid. < > Who're you? < > You deaf?

DOODLE. I'm Doodle.

MARJORAM. Kinda name is that?

DOODLE. A nick.

MARJORAM. What?

DOODLE. A *nick*name.

TOPH. He's the new kid.

MARJORAM. Don't you think I know that? < > Welcome to the quad. Reno-Teeno showing you the lay of the land?

RENO. Marjoram, just go home.

MARJORAM. Can't I make friends too?

RENO. Doodle—don't listen to her. She's ...

MARJORAM. I'm what? What am I?

RENO. < > Nothing.

MARJORAM. So. Doodle. You're Reno's new friend, huh?

DOODLE. Um, we just met, so—

MARJORAM. Didn't Reno tell you? About his problem.

RENO. I don't have a problem, Majoram! Just go home.

MARJORAM. Reno's gay.

RENO. I am not! Shut *up*, you stupid little idiot!

MARJORAM. Hey now—enough name calling. You don't want to get in trouble with the old man, right Reno?

RENO. You better just go home or I'll tell him what you said and he'll make you swallow—

MARJORAM *(overlapping)*. He'll make you swallow three pumpkins at the same time. Can it, Reno-bambino.

RENO. Keep calling me names and see what happens.

MARJORAM. Pansy. < > Doofus. < > Homo. < > See. Nothing. Do it, Toph. *(Pushes TOPH.)* Go.

TOPH *(hesitantly)*. Pansy. *(Runs back to MARJORAM.)*

MARJORAM. Keep going.

(TOPH goes back to RENO.)

TOPH. Doofus. < > HOMO!

MARJORAM *(laughs)*. Nice. Hey Doodle … did Reno *make* you wear that dress or what?

TOPH. Maybe he's a *gay* too.

DOODLE. No. No. < > He made me. I didn't wanna wear it. *(Takes off the dress.)*

MARJORAM. That's what I thought. You don't look like— well, you look normal.

RENO *(to MARJORAM)*. I hate you.

(MARJORAM laughs. TOPH laughs. DOODLE laughs ...
sort of.)

RENO *(cont'd)*. Shut up! You're all stupid, stupid ... morons and, and ... you don't know anything ... about anything! I hate you all!

MARJORAM. Are you gonna go cry to the old man now?

TOPH. Yeah. What's 'a matter, Reno? You scared?

MARJORAM. I think I want that dress.

TOPH. Maybe you should take it.

MARJORAM. That's the first good idea you've had.

TOPH. Thanks.

MARJORAM. You wanna give it to me and make this easy?

RENO. Just leave me alone, OK? Tomboys don't wear tutus.

MARJORAM. What did you call me?

(MARJORAM rips off RENO's tutu, pushing him to the
ground. RENO does not resist. MARJORAM puts on the
tutu, giggles. A light comes on upstairs. TOPH and
MARJORAM hide.)

BAUMGARTNER *(offstage)*. Reno? Is everything all right?

RENO. Everything's ... yeah ... everything's *normal*.

(RENO and DOODLE exchange a look. RENO exits.
DOODLE looks around, takes off the bandana and slinks
back into his apartment. VALENCIA is lounging diva
style on the countertop.)

VALENCIA. Hola hola. I can no wait to taste this king-
sized Peanut Cupper Reese's Butt.

DOODLE. Reese's Peanut Butter Cup.

VALENCIA. BAH—

DOODLE. ¡Bahfoogee! Get outta here, Valencia. I'm not in
the mood. I feel sick to my stomach.

VALENCIA. Too much PayDay.

DOODLE. Just go.

VALENCIA. What's wrong, *glo-o-o-o-o-o-my* Doodle?
Where's the candy?

DOODLE. There is none.

VALENCIA. What happened?

DOODLE. I think I did a bad thing.

VALENCIA. ¿Cómo?

DOODLE. It wasn't my fault.

VALENCIA. You can tell the Valencia.

DOODLE. I think I might have to swallow pumpkins.

(A knock on the door. DOODLE freezes.)

VALENCIA. The troll! Oh no!

(Another knock.)

MARJORAM & TOPH. Dooooooooodle! Trick-or-treat!

DOODLE. ¡Pa´ arriba! Your hiding place!

VALENCIA. No, por favor, don't make me go in there!
You always forgetting Valencia when she goes into hiding.

DOODLE. It's the kids I just met.

VALENCIA. What? You are embarrassed of the Valencia?

(Knocking!)

DOODLE. If they find out I have an imaginary goat—

VALENCIA. You *are* embarrassed of the Valencia!

DOODLE. ¡Por favor, Valencia!

(Knocking!!!!! VALENCIA mopes and jumps inside the mirror hanging on the wall, disappears. DOODLE opens the door. No one is there.)

DOODLE *(cont'd)*. Hello?
MARJORAM & TOPH *(jumping out)*. AAAAAHHHHHHH!
DOODLE. AAAAAAHHHHHHHHHHHHHHHHHHHH!
TOPH. Hiya, Doodle noodle.

(TOPH and MARJORAM enter the apartment uninvited.)

MARJORAM. Whoa. This place sucks.
TOPH. Yeah. It sucks.
MARJORAM. Don't say that word.
DOODLE *(looks up to the window, then closes the door)*. Um, we haven't unpacked yet…
MARJORAM *(looks through all the cabinets)*. Got anything good to eat?

(TOPH checks himself out in the mirror. VALENCIA jumps up, makes a chupacabra face. TOPH sees her.)

TOPH. AAAAHHHH!

(DOODLE laughs.)

MARJORAM. Why you freaking out, little bro?
TOPH. Um, um … it was a … it's nothing.
MARJORAM *(to DOODLE)*. What's so funny?
DOODLE. Nothing.
TOPH. Um, hey Doodle, you got any delicious Halloween candy?
DOODLE. I have PayDays!

TOPH. GROSS! Who eats PayDays? That's like the worst candy bar ever invented ever.

DOODLE. Oh. They're mi mamá's.

MARJORAM. Mamá, huh? Are you an alien?

TOPH *(alien voice)*. My name is Doodle and I am from the planet Ooodle Ooodle Ooodle.

MARJORAM. No, idiot. Like from another country.

DOODLE. Mamá is … no, we were born here.

MARJORAM. You don't sound very American.

TOPH. Our dad says aliens are taking all the jobs.

DOODLE. Pues, tu papá es un estúpido.

MARJORAM. What'd you say?

DOODLE. I say … aliens only take … the crappy jobs. Like convenience stores.

TOPH. Yeah. Convenience stores.

MARJORAM. Do you have any food? *Besides* PayDays.

TOPH. It's OK, the last kid who lived in this apartment was really poor too.

(VALENCIA makes angry faces in the mirror behind TOPH.)

DOODLE. We're not poor! Papá is still—we're in transition. That's what Mamá says.

MARJORAM. Why are you hanging out with Reno?

DOODLE. He's nice, I guess—

TOPH. He's kinda weird.

MARJORAM. Trust me. You don't want to hang out with the wrong crowd here. Reno's trouble.

DOODLE. He seems OK.

TOPH. He made you wear a dress.

DOODLE. Just for Halloween.

MARJORAM. Not for Reno. Reno takes dress-up *very* seriously.

TOPH. You sure you're not an alien?

DOODLE. I'm from Earth. *(Imitating TOPH's alien voice.)* No Doodle oodle noodle.

(DOODLE and TOPH invent a robot alien dance.)

MARJORAM. Hey, morons, let's pull a Halloween prank!

TOPH. I like pranks.

MARJORAM. We'll have to be very quiet.

DOODLE. Because of the troll?

MARJORAM. You don't believe that stuff, do you?

DOODLE. No.

MARJORAM. You should.

TOPH. Really?

MARJORAM. Yeah really. < > You know about the blood pumpkins?

DOODLE. Just what Reno said—

MARJORAM. They're filled with the blood of kids who lived in *this* apartment.

(VALENCIA is very concerned.)

MARJORAM *(cont'd)*. D'you hear him using that machine thingy?

(MARJORAM imitates the grinding sound. MARJORAM nods. TOPH nods. VALENCIA is terrified.)

MARJORAM *(cont'd)*. But, I know something that might save you.

(VALENCIA is excited.)

MARJORAM *(cont'd)*. Aren't you interested?

(VALENCIA nods fervently.)

DOODLE. OK. Sure. Whatever.
MARJORAM. We have to shake the trees till all the blood
    pumpkins fall to the ground.
DOODLE. What's that supposed to do?
MARJORAM. No more pumpkins, no more problems.
TOPH. Come on, Doodle, it'll be fun! Bloody pumpkin guts
    everywhere!

*(TOPH opens the door. Wind rushes in. He and MAR-
JORAM dash into the courtyard.)*

TOPH. You coming, *(Alien voice.)* Doodle ooodle noodle?

(VALENCIA makes a chupacabra face at TOPH.)

TOPH *(cont'd)*. AHHH!

*(TOPH scurries out. DOODLE looks to VALENCIA.
DOODLE goes into the courtyard and VALENCIA van-
ishes in the mirror.)*

MARJORAM. The trick is to be perfectly quiet.

*(TOPH rushes over to one of the trees, shakes it slightly.
A few orbs fall. He giggles.)*

MARJORAM *(cont'd)*. Toph. Shut up. *(Shakes a tree. More orbs fall.)*
TOPH. Come on!

(DOODLE hesitantly shakes the tree. TOPH joins. MAR-JORAM joins. Orange orbs flood the courtyard. A few beats of anxious silence.)

MARJORAM. PUMPKIN THIEF! PUMPKIN THIEF! PUMPKIN THIEF! *(Hurls orbs at DOODLE.)*
DOODLE. ¿Qué? ¡Ay, cállate! Shhh! ¡ Párale!
TOPH. PUMPKIN THIEF! PUMPKIN THIEF! PUMPKIN THIEF!

(DOODLE runs into the apartment. An offstage noise. MARJORAM and TOPH dash off. Some silence. DOO-DLE looks out the window. BAUMGARTNER, wearing his fumigating mask, grumbles into the courtyard wield-ing a rake. DOODLE gasps. BAUMGARTNER surveys the damage, sees DOODLE in the window. DOODLE gasps again, ducks down. BAUMGARTNER sees the trail of orbs leading to DOODLE's door. He picks one up. It's dripping red. He knocks on DOODLE's door. VALEN-CIA pops up. DOODLE motions for her to stay down. Knock. DOODLE peeks out the window. DOODLE is perfectly still. BAUMGARTNER opens the door.)

DOODLE *(screaming)*. AAAAAAAAHHHHHHHHH!
BAUMGARTNER *(screaming back)*. BWWWAAAAHHH!

(DOODLE runs and hides in an open moving box. VA-LENCIA is perfectly still, mimicking a painting. BAUM-GARTNER stomps over to the box, opens it.)

BAUMGARTNER *(cont'd)*. Are you the one who shook my trees?

DOODLE. ¡No, por favor!

BAUMGARTNER. Then why are you hiding?

DOODLE. ¡Por favor, no me lleves!

BAUMGARTNER. I'm not going to *take* you. Why would I take you?

DOODLE. Because you're a troll and Mamá owes you money!

BAUMGARTNER. Where is your mother?

DOODLE. 7-Eleven.

BAUMGARTNER. Your father?

DOODLE. Por favor, don't make me swallow pumpkins!

BAUMGARTNER. Come out of that box.

DOODLE. No, gracias. I think I'll stay here.

BAUMGARTNER. We need to talk about my trees.

DOODLE. Lo siento, Señor Ogro. I'm really really really really sorry for shaking your trees.

BAUMGARTNER. So it *was* you.

DOODLE. ¡Ay, no! Not *just* me.

BAUMGARTNER. Let me guess—Marjoram and Toph?

DOODLE. They *made* me.

BAUMGARTNER. They *made* you?

DOODLE. That's right.

BAUMGARTNER. You didn't shake my trees willingly?

DOODLE. No exactamente …

BAUMGARTNER. Come out of that box.

DOODLE. If I'm in here and you're out there, then no pumpkins get in my belly.

BAUMGARTNER. Pumpkins?

DOODLE. Por favor, Señor Ogro, I'm really sorry for everything I did.

BAUMGARTNER. Tell me what it is you've done.

DOODLE *(fast)*. I left the apartment without Mamá's permission, I wore a dress, I told a lie, I said a curse and I shook your trees—*willingly*.

BAUMGARTNER. You've been busy.

DOODLE. And now you want to make me swallow your pumpkins porque that's what happens to evil niños in this quadruplex.

BAUMGARTNER *(takes off his mask)*. See? You're safe. Come out of the box. Please.

DOODLE *(slowly exits the box)*. Why do you wear that mask? And that suit?

BAUMGARTNER. Protection.

DOODLE. Protection against what?

BAUMGARTNER. Fumes from the chemicals I spray on the trees.

DOODLE. You mean the blood of evil ninos! *(Makes for the box.)*

BAUMGARTNER. No, no … My boy, what is your name?

DOODLE. I don't think I should tell you.

BAUMGARTNER. Why ever not?

DOODLE. Well … isn't there some kind of rule? If a troll knows your name, then—

BAUMGARTNER. There's no rule.

DOODLE. < > Me llamo Doodle.

BAUMGARTNER. Reno told me about what happened with you.

DOODLE. Oh no—

BAUMGARTNER. Interesting moniker. Doodle. That's what it's called when a cat misses—

DOODLE. Misses the litter box. Sí, I know.

BAUMGARTNER. A doodle is also something you draw without thinking.

DOODLE. I do a lot of things without thinking.

BAUMGARTNER. Is that why you're called Doodle?

DOODLE. Maybe. I think Mamá likes the way it sounds.

BAUMGARTNER. We should discuss my oranges.

DOODLE. You mean pumpkins?

BAUMGARTNER. Pumpkins are of the genus Cucurbita.

DOODLE. Cook my what!?

BAUMGARTNER. They grow on vines. Not trees. These are oranges.

DOODLE. I knew it. Reno said they were pumpkins.

BAUMGARTNER. He was getting your goat.

DOODLE. He met my goat.

BAUMGARTNER. No—*getting* your goat—

DOODLE. No, enserio, he *actually saw* her.

BAUMGARTNER. Who?

DOODLE. My goat.

BAUMGARTNER. You have an actual goat?

DOODLE. Sí.

BAUMGARTNER. In this apartment?

DOODLE. Sí.

BAUMGARTNER. Your mother did not pay a pet deposit.

DOODLE. She's imaginary.

BAUMGARTNER. Your mother?

DOODLE. My goat!

BAUMGARTNER. Ahhhhh. *(Peels an orange, reveals the blood red inside.)* My *oranges* are delicious. Take a bite. You'll see.

DOODLE. Oh, no no no! That's what all trolls say when they want the kid to eat the poison fruit.

BAUMGARTNER. It's not poison.

DOODLE. But they are rojas. Oranges are not red. That's why they're called oranges. Because they are orange.
BAUMGARTNER. Taste it.
DOODLE. How do I know it's not poison?
BAUMGARTNER *(eats a slice)*. See? Try it.
DOODLE. You could have immunity to the poison.
BAUMGARTNER. Trust me. They're not poison.

(DOODLE takes a slice.)

BAUMGARTNER *(cont'd)*. Go ahead.

(DOODLE eats it.)

BAUMGARTNER *(cont'd)*. Pretty tasty, huh?
DOODLE. Hmmm. It tastes like … sabe como … like wind and sunshine. *(Takes another slice.)* ¡Qué rico! *(Takes another.)*

BAUMGARTNER. Slow down.

(DOODLE takes another.)

BAUMGARTNER *(cont'd)*. Whoa!
DOODLE. Perdon, I'm kinda hungry.
BAUMGARTNER. Eat slower. You'll get a tummy ache.

(DOODLE shoots BAUMGARTNER a suspicious look.)

BAUMGARTNER *(cont'd)*. *From eating too fast!* < > This is a hybrid orange I've been developing. It's a cross between giant grapefruit—*Citrus paradisi*—and a Spanish blood orange—*Citrus sinensis*.

DOODLE. So, you're not a troll?

BAUMGARTNER. I'm a retired botanist.

DOODLE. Is that some type of troll?

BAUMGARTNER. No—I study plants. Citrus precisely. I look for unique features in plants. Things that make them different from the rest. And when I find those things, well … I celebrate them.

DOODLE. I *knew* you weren't a troll.

BAUMGARTNER. If you *knew*, why did you hide in that box?

DOODLE. Maybe I didn't know *for sure*. Reno is very convincing.

BAUMGARTNER. Reno has an active imagination. He likes to tell stories. He's my nieto.

DOODLE. Your grandson?

BAUMGARTNER. That's right.

DOODLE. < > Hey … Señor … um …

BAUMGARTNER. Señor Baumgartner.

DOODLE. Bomb Gardener … do you know if Reno … is Reno angry with me?

BAUMGARTNER. You should ask him that question.

DOODLE. Maybe. < > Why does Reno call you a troll?

BAUMGARTNER. Reno feels safer if I'm a troll.

DOODLE. It doesn't bother you to be called a troll?

BAUMGARTNER. If Reno feels safer, then, no, it doesn't bother me. < > What's your *real* name, Doodle?

DOODLE. Martín.

BAUMGARTNER. That's a very grown-up name.

DOODLE. It's Papá's name.

BAUMGARTNER. It's a very nice name. Maybe you should use it.

DOODLE. Mamá used to call me Martín whenever I was in trouble. < > But now it makes her sad to say it. Ever since Papá ...

BAUMGARTNER. Oh. I see. < > You know, you and Reno have something in common.

DOODLE. No, Reno likes to wear girls' clothes.

BAUMGARTNER. That's just a costume.

DOODLE. No, that's who Reno *is*. He doesn't just wear dresses on Halloween.

BAUMGARTNER. He told you that?

DOODLE. Yeah.

BAUMGARTNER. Hunh. < > I didn't mean you were similar because of how you dress. < > Reno lost his father too. And his mother. That's why he lives with me.

DOODLE. Bahfoogee.

BAUMGARTNER. What?

DOODLE. Bahfoogee. It's a curse word.

(BAUMGARTNER grumbles.)

DOODLE *(cont'd)*. In goat. You say it when something is lost.

BAUMGARTNER. < > I like it.

DOODLE. Señor Bomb Gardener—I didn't *lose* my father. He is ... he was sent back.

BAUMGARTNER. I see.

DOODLE. Please don't tell anybody.

BAUMGARTNER. Trolls are very good at keeping secrets.

(DOODLE fetches the envelope of money from the cabinet and hands it to BAUMGARTNER.)

DOODLE. It's the rent. Mamá asked me to give it to you.

BAUMGARTNER. Thank you. < > We should discuss the consequences for shaking my trees.

DOODLE. Lay it on me.

BAUMGARTNER. There are several baskets in the courtyard. Put all the oranges in them. Take a couple out. Para tu mamá.

DOODLE. You won't tell her about the trees?

BAUMGARTNER. What you meant as a prank was actually very helpful. The oranges are obviously ripe and ready to eat. You saved this old troll hours of ups and downs on that rickety ladder.

(DOODLE and BAUMGARTNER shake hands and BAUM-GARTNER exits. VALENCIA jumps out of the mirror.)

VALENCIA. Ay, is so very bo-o-o-o-o-ring in there, Doodle Pequeño.

DOODLE. Maybe you shouldn't call me that anymore.

VALENCIA. WAIT! Did the troll place a curse on you like he did his pumpkins?

DOODLE. He's not a troll! He's a grandpa. And those aren't pumpkins. They're oranges. Things aren't always what they seem. < > I got a job to do. Wanna help?

VALENCIA. I can no go outside—

DOODLE. You can hold onto me.

VALENCIA. You promise not to be letting go?

DOODLE. Sí, te lo prometo.

(DOODLE opens the door. A gust of wind. VALENCIA jumps on DOODLE's back.)

VALENCIA. I hold on very tight.
DOODLE. Maybe not *so* tight.

(VALENCIA and DOODLE enter the courtyard.)

DOODLE *(cont'd)*. I can't do this job with a goat on my back. I have an idea.

(DOODLE and VALENCIA go to a tree.)

DOODLE *(cont'd)*. Hold this. It has roots and isn't going anywhere.
VALENCIA. Are you sure?
DOODLE. Sí, estoy seguro. *(Guides VALENCIA to hold the tree.)* You good?
VALENCIA. No, but I'll be a brave Valencia!
DOODLE *(finds the basket and begins to work. Sings to comfort VALENCIA)*.
    NARANJA DULCE
    LIMÓN PARTIDO
    DAME UN ABRAZO
    QUE YO TE PIDO.

DOODLE & VALENCIA.
    SI FUERAN FALSOS
    MIS JURAMENTOS,
    EN UN MOMENTO
    SE OLVIDARÁN.

(DOODLE works for a few moments before RENO enters. He is no longer wearing the vampire makeup or costume. He is now wearing an everyday dress.)

VALENCIA. Reno like the city in Nevada returns!

(DOODLE stands. Silence. Then RENO and DOODLE speak simultaneously.)

RENO. I'm sorry for—   DOODLE. I am sorry—
DOODLE. You're sorry?
RENO. I shouldn't have made you wear the dress.
DOODLE. You didn't *make* me. I said that because of the other kids. I wore it porque … I thought we could be amigos. < > Sorry about your tutu.
RENO. It's cool. I've got lots more.
DOODLE. ¡Esos cabritos son unos pingos!
RENO. What?
DOODLE. Pingos.
RENO. Pingos?
DOODLE. That's right. Punks. Those kids are punks.
RENO. Pingos. Cool. Reno spoke Spanish. < > Hey, you need help?

(DOODLE offers RENO a basket. They pick up the oranges. DOODLE starts to sing. RENO listens and tries to join in.)

DOODLE.   RENO.
NARANJA DULCE
LIMÓN PARTIDO
DAME UN ABRAZO   … UN ABRAZO
QUE YO TE PIDO.   … YO TE PIDO.

SI FUERAN FALSOS   SI … FALSOS
MIS JURAMENTOS,   MIS … MENTOS,
EN UN MOMENTO   … UN MOMENTO
SE OLVIDARÁN.   SE … DARÁN.

.

(A big wind blows. VALENCIA floats a little.)

VALENCIA. Ooooh, I starting to feel a little light in the head.

(A light comes on in another window. MARJORAM and TOPH lean out the lit window.)

MARJORAM. Oh, look, Toph. It's Reno-Homo and Doodle Dandy doing a little late-night gardening.

TOPH. Yeah. Gardening.

DOODLE. Hey!

TOPH. Hey yourself!

DOODLE. You can't talk to us that way anymore.

RENO. Yeah … pingos!

TOPH *(to MARJORAM)*. What's a pingo?

MARJORAM. Shut up. You're both homos!

TOPH. What's a homo?

MARJORAM. Shut up.

DOODLE. ¿Y qué? So what if we are? What are you going to do about it?

RENO. Doodle—

MARJORAM. Don't make me come out there!

DOODLE. If you do, then you better be ready to fight us both! And just so you know, I'm a black belt in Tae Kwon Do. *(Strikes a pose.)*

TOPH. What's Tae Kwon Do?

MARJORAM. Come on!

(MARJORAM and TOPH disappear from the window.)

RENO. This is not good.

VALENCIA. No good.

DOODLE. Hold your ground.
RENO. Are you really a black belt?
DOODLE. Not at all.
VALENCIA. Ay.

> *(A few moments pass. DOODLE and RENO stand back-to-back, ready to be ambushed. MARJORAM and TOPH come out of nowhere, lobbing Sweet Tarts.)*

TOPH & MARJORAM. Sweet Tarts for the sweethearts!

> *(Sweet Tart war! TOPH and MARJORAM back DOODLE and RENO into a corner. When they run out of Sweet Tarts, they hurl oranges. When they run out of oranges, the kids standoff.)*

DOODLE. Just leave us alone!
MARJORAM. Aren't they cute, Toph?
TOPH. Yeah, *Princess* Peg-leg and *Countess* Chaos.
DOODLE. Get out of here! This is our courtyard. *(Picks up an orange.)*
MARJORAM. Oh, look, Toph—Doodle's got a blood pumpkin. So scary!
DOODLE. I'll make you swallow it!
RENO (picks up an orange). Yeah.
DOODLE *(picks up another orange)*. And then another one.
RENO *(picks up another orange)*. And another one …
DOODLE & RENO. AND ANOTHER ONE!!!

> *(DOODLE and RENO charge, DOODLE wrestling MARJORAM to the ground, RENO wrestling TOPH. They begin to cram the oranges into TOPH and MARJORAM's mouths.)*

TOPH. Get off me, you stupid vampire!

MARJORAM. Boys cannot hit girls! Boys cannot hit girls!

(During the battle, a gust of wind lifts VALENCIA to the top of the tree. BAUMGARTNER roars in, full nuclear suit, carrying his sprayer.)

BAUMGARTNER. BWAAHHHHHHHHHHHHHHHHH!

(The kids jump to their feet. TOPH screams with an orange in his mouth. BAUMGARTNER backs them into a corner.)

BAUMGARTNER *(cont'd)*. Who dares to eat my blood pumpkins? < > Answer me! This old troll will not be toyed with! *(Holds the sprayer wand close to their faces.)*

TOPH *(spitting out the orange)*. I'm-Toph-please-don't-eat-me!

MARJORAM *(spitting out the orange)*. Marjoram, but you already know that, old man.

BAUMGARTNER. < > And who are you, young man?

DOODLE. I'm ... I'm ... Martín.

BAUMGARTNER. Martín, huh? < > Well, you're *all* trespassers! < > There's only one thing I can think of as punishment. *(Growls.)*

RENO. Grandpa, stop.

BAUMGARTNER. Quiet! The troll is thinking of punishments! *(Growl.)*

RENO. No, Grandpa. There's no troll. *(Lifts BAUMGARTNER's mask.)* It's just you and me. You asked me not to wear my dresses outside of the apartment but I did it anyway. I'm sorry. Toph, Marjoram … I'm sorry we crammed oranges down your throat. Come on, Grandpa … let's go.

DOODLE. Wait. < > You shouldn't apologize.

RENO. It's OK, Doodle—we shouldn't have fought back. It only makes it worse.

BAUMGARTNER. That's right.

MARJORAM. Just wait till we tell our dad—oh, he's gonna be fierce!

RENO. I said I was sorry.

DOODLE. No! Stop saying that. You shouldn't be sorry. These pingos are the ones who should be apologizing. They can't just call you names 'cause you're different.

RENO. Doodle—

DOODLE. They can't just steal your clothes and … trespass in your courtyard!

MARJORAM. We're not trespassing, god!

DOODLE. They can't kick you out 'cause you're different. This is your home too, Reno. *You don't have to apologize.*

BAUMGARTNER. < > He's right. You shouldn't have to apologize.

RENO. OK. Well. Then. I'm *not sorry* for wearing a dress.

DOODLE. Sí, tienes razón.

RENO. I'm not sorry at all!

MARJORAM. Oh my god. YAWN. Toph, let's go.

RENO. At least I'm brave enough to be who I am, Marjoram.

MARJORAM. Who are you? *What* are you?

RENO. I'm Reno. Like the city in Nevada.

(MARJORAM laughs.)

RENO *(cont'd)*. I remember how those girls at school picked on you last year. They called you those names—

MARJORAM. Can it, Reno!

RENO. You didn't have to be embarrassed.

MARJORAM. Reno—I'm warning you—

RENO. You don't have to be afraid, Marj—

MARJORAM. Stop it! *(Stepping closer.)* If your troll-grandpa wasn't here, you wouldn't be so brave.

TOPH. Leave him alone, Marj.

MARJORAM. Shut up, you little … pingo.

TOPH. How come you're so mean *all* the time?

MARJORAM. Keep talking and I'll show you mean!

TOPH. You're so gay!

(MARJORAM is speechless. She looks to RENO.)

MARJORAM. Toph, that's not … you shouldn't … *(Looks to BAUMGARTNER. She heads offstage.)*

TOPH. Marj—wait. Marj—I didn't mean it! I don't even know what gay is.

MARJORAM *(turning back)*. Toph … just don't say that word, OK?

TOPH. Is it a swear word or something?

MARJORAM. It's not a swear. It just hurts like one.

RENO. It doesn't have to hurt, Marj.

MARJORAM. Yeah, well … he shouldn't say it, OK?

TOPH. But you said it.

MARJORAM. That was different.

TOPH. How?

MARJORAM. It just was! < > Come on. Let's go. Halloween's over. *(Almost offstage.)* Hey Reno! That dress is so … that dress is … that dress …

(MARJORAM and TOPH exit.)

RENO *(to DOODLE)*. Thanks for sticking up for me like that.

DOODLE. I wish I could be that brave all the time.

RENO. You are, Martín. Grandpa told me you ate the oranges. Even though you thought they were blood pumpkins, you still ate 'em. That's brave. < > It's official. Welcome to the quad.

(DOODLE and RENO shake hands.)

RENO. There's no more troll, Grandpa.

BAUMGARTNER. Those kids won't stop what they're doing.

DOODLE. Señor Bomb Gardener, we'll do it like Papá says … un día a la vez.

RENO. Huh?

BAUMGARTNER. One day at a time.

VALENCIA. B-ah-ah-ah-ah-ah-ah-ah!

DOODLE. What are you doing up there?

(Wind.)

BAUMGARTNER. Who's he talking to?

RENO. His goat.

BAUMGARTNER. Oh. Right.

VALENCIA. Is time for me to go.

DOODLE. Pero—

VALENCIA. Once I am letting go of this branch, I riding the Santa Ana winds.

DOODLE. Where will you go, Valencia?

VALENCIA. When someone need me, they grabbing me by the horns, just like you.

(DOODLE tosses an orange up to VALENCIA. BAUM-GARTNER looks for it to fall back. It never does.)
DOODLE. Don't forget me, por favor.
VALENCIA. Imposible, mi Martín.

(The Santa Ana blows hard and the wind chimes fill the Halloween air. VALENCIA floats away, framed by the bronzed, full moon. DOODLE—now Martín—stares at the sky until VALENCIA is gone.)

DOODLE. BAAAAHHHFOOOGEEEE!
RENO. BAAAAHHHFOOOGEEEE!
DOODLE & RENO. BAAAAHHHFOOOGEEEE!

THE END

DISCUSSION QUESTIONS

The following questions are intended to help guide a discussion about the characters, relationships and events in *The Transition of Doodle Pequeño*. They are designed to inspire a dialogue that extends beyond the walls of the theatre by providing audience members the opportunity to reflect while rehearsing the challenging and important conversations that the play may stimulate.

These questions can be adapted for many ages and contexts, including post-show discussions facilitated at the theatre, and reflections between teachers and students or between parents and children. Of course, they can also be a guide for children to talk to each other about the play. Though the children will probably have better questions for one another and the characters than we could ever imagine!

—Abra Chusid, Dramaturg

QUESTIONS TO ENGAGE

What is this play about?

With a friend, retell the story of the play. When were your versions of the story the same? When were they different? Why do you think there are differences in your versions?

Draw a picture of some of your favorite moments or images from the play. Why do these moments stand out?

QUESTIONS FOR ACTIVE REFLECTION

When is there a moment in the play that you empathized with a character? Did you ever feel conflicting viewpoints based on your own experiences?

In the play, many people and objects are discovered to be different than they first seemed—pumpkins are really oranges and a scary troll is really a caring grandfather. In life, too, our first impressions often change as we gain more information. Have you ever met someone who is different than they seemed at first? What new information changed your first impression?

During the play, Doodle learns to speak out against bullying, a feat requiring great courage. Why is it sometimes hard to speak out against actions like bullying? When is a time you felt courageous, and similar to Doodle, you spoke up against something wrong or unjust?

Valencia teaches Doodle and Reno to say "Bahfoogee"" a word with many meanings. How does the use of "Bahfoogee" change throughout the play? What does it mean to you when Reno and Doodle say it at the very end of the play?

Other words with multiple meanings become hurtful when spoken as swears. What are some of the words that hurt Reno's feelings? Why do you think they are hurtful? How can we become more aware of the effects of the words and labels we use?

There's a lot of talk in schools about bully prevention, yet it continues to happen. If you could change one thing to stop bullying in your school, what would that be?

Naranja Dulce

VALENCIA: "No, but I'll be a brave Valencia!"

Traditional Mexican Song

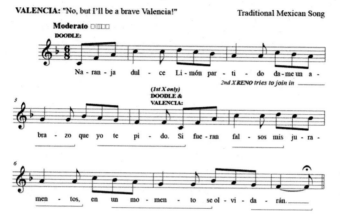

Na - ran - ja dul - ce Li - món par - ti - do da - me un a -
bra - zo que yo te pi - do. Si fue - ran fal - sos mis ju - ra -
men - tos, en un mo - men - to se ol - vi - da - rán.

Dialogue cue
RENO: "Pingos. Cool. Reno spoke Spanish. < > Hey, you need help?"

Music - D.C. al Fine

(DOODLE starts to sing. RENO listens and tries to join in.)

NOTES